TAKING TEA

With Alice

Looking-Glass Tea Parties and Fanciful Victorian Teas

DAWN HYLTON GOTTLIEB & DIANE SEDO
FOREWORD BY EDWARD WAKELING AND ANNE CLARK AMOR

WARNER 🅦 TREASURES®
PUBLISHED BY WARNER BOOKS
A TIME WARNER COMPANY

Warner Treasures® name and logo are registered trademarks of Warner Books, Inc.

1271 Avenue of the Americas, New York, NY 10020

Visit our Web site at http://pathfinder.com/twep

Ⓦ A Time Warner Company

Printed in Singapore
First Printing: October 1997
10 9 8 7 6 5 4 3 2 1

ISBN: 0-446-91173-9

Book design by Flamur Tonuzi
Photography by Kathryn Russell
Photo styling by Sunday Hendrickson
Food styling by Diane Elander
Illustrations by Darlene Jones
Vintage clothing courtesy of Palace Costume Company
Holiday Yuletide clothing courtesy of Sandra Johnson

This book is dedicated to our mothers,

*who taught us the importance of being a true friend
and how a lifetime of memories can begin
sharing thoughts
over a lovely cup of tea.*

Contents

Foreword
Lewis Carroll and Tea with the Real Alice

Lewis Carroll was, to all intents and purposes, an entertainer, either as a storyteller or as a puzzler. He loved to see the expressions of concentration and fascination on the faces of his young friends as he wove a story to delight them. Most of his stories were made up on the spur of the moment, but good stories were often repeated. As a mathematician, he was keen to make this subject a pleasurable experience for children, and he endeavored to produce games and puzzles that would provide them with fun and excitement, but also develop their powers of thinking and reasoning.

When the real Alice was growing up in Victorian England, the children of rich families were not allowed to take their meals with the grown-ups. Instead they ate in the nursery or schoolroom. But Lewis Carroll preferred the company of children to adults, and nothing pleased him better than taking tea with Alice and her sisters. Sometimes he was invited into the schoolroom at the Deanery by the three little girls, and joined in their meal, making a dinner of their tea.

On other occasions, their governess brought the girls over to Carroll's rooms in the College, where he gave them their tea. He invariably provided their favorite food, and brewed the tea himself, walking up and down and swinging the teapot from side to side for exactly ten minutes to make sure it was properly infused.

Best of all were their river trips on summer afternoons. Carroll, in white flannels and a straw boater, always brought the picnic hamper. Cold chicken, salad, and cakes were the usual fare. Often they landed at Nuneham, and took tea in a picnic hut, using plates and cutlery borrowed from a riverside cottage. "To us the hut might have been a Fairy King's palace, and the picnic a banquet in our honour," recalled Alice many years later.

Sometimes they boiled a kettle under a haycock and brewed tea, or drank lemonade or ginger beer.

But whenever they took tea together, there were sure to be games and stories and lots of fun. *Taking Tea with Alice* is a wonderful source of ideas to recapture the Victorians' delight in tea parties and games on the lawn. There are many delicious recipes and lots of entertaining games for children of all ages. Now, with the help of this delightful book, modern children can enjoy their own wonderland of fun, games, and party food by *Taking Tea with Alice.*

Edward Wakeling
Editor, *Lewis Carroll's Diaries*

Anne Clark Amor
Author, *The Real Alice*

ALICE PLEASANCE LIDDELL—
the Real-Life Alice in Wonderland

Alice Pleasance Liddell lived an unusually privileged life. Born in England in 1852 during Queen Victoria's reign (1837–1901) and named after a princess, Alice lived with her family in the Dean's private residence, called the Deanery, at Oxford University. Her mother, Lorina Hannah Liddell, and father, Henry George Liddell, Dean of Christ Church, would have the unique advantage of receiving frequent social calls from the world's finest artists, scholars, mathematicians, photographers, and writers. On April 26, 1856, when Alice was nearly four years old, she met Charles Lutwidge Dodgson (Lewis Carroll), a twenty-four-year-old mathematics lecturer who taught (and lived) at the university. Dodgson, comfortable around the young, quickly became friends with the Liddell sisters, Lorina, Alice, and Edith.

Through the years he would frequently call upon the three girls to painstakingly pose for a series of photographs, as photography was extremely new and quite a novelty in mid-nineteenth-century England. As Alice grew older and her friendship with Mr. Dodgson developed, unlike the average Victorian girl who would "speak only when spoken to," Alice's wit, imagination, and spirit inspired Charles Dodgson to write the *Alice* stories.

Alice loved the arts and the math and word games she and Mr. Dodgson would play. But most of all, Alice loved Mr. Dodgson's stories; "Let's pretend" were Alice's favorite words. One hot fourth of July day in 1862, as they quietly guided their boat up the River Thames (or Isis, as it was known to those who lived at Oxford), Dodgson and his friend Mr. Duckworth manned the oars as they rowed to their destination, a picnic on the bank of the Thames. On this "golden afternoon," Dodgson tenderly told the wide-eyed Alice, Lorina, and Edith Liddell the first of many extraordinary tales of "Alice's Adventures Under Ground" (later to be published as *Alice's Adventures in Wonderland,* in 1865).

This special day marked the beginning of a story that lives on as the third most frequently read book in the world. The first is the Bible; the second, the works of Shakespeare. To be third in this literary circle is an extraordinary accomplishment indeed.

Alice and her sisters never attended school as their brother, Harry, did, but were educated at home in the nursery by their governess, Miss Prickett, or "Pricks," as she was affectionately called. Because Miss Prickett was not proficient at every subject (such as French and singing), the services of other teachers were engaged. When Alice was seventeen, John Ruskin, the famous artist and writer, was hired as an art instructor to teach her drawing and painting. And because Mrs. Liddell always made sure that her family had the best of everything, all of her girls were fashionably dressed at all times. A seamstress was hired to sew three identical dresses for the sisters, with frills, pleats, and lace that took the servants hours to iron. On outings, Mrs. Liddell insisted that the girls dress properly, including the wearing of matching hats and gloves. Teatime was also of the utmost importance, and the girls spent many an hour eating scones and jam as they enjoyed the charms of "taking tea," whether it be in the nursery or, when the weather would comply with their wishes, out-of-doors.

As Alice grew older, she saw Mr. Dodgson less and less frequently, as he continued to fall in and out of favor with Mrs. Liddell. When Alice was twenty, Queen Victoria sent her son Prince Leopold to study at Christ Church, and he frequently visited the Liddells. Alice fell in love with the prince, but was unable to marry him, as the queen insisted her sons marry princesses. Brokenhearted, Alice then met Reginald Hargreaves, another student at the university, whom she married in a glorious wedding ceremony at Westminster Abbey. Alice and Regi went on to live in an enormous mansion, where they had three sons, Alan, Rex, and Caryl.

Dodgson remained a bachelor and continued to live at Christ Church his entire life, and is still considered one of England's finest photographers of children. Twenty years Alice's senior, Charles Lutwidge Dodgson had many other child friends long after Alice grew to adulthood, but no other child ever inspired him more, no other child did he love more, than Alice, his "Dream Child."

Imagine . . .

. . . what life must have been like for Alice Liddell,
Lewis Carroll's real-life Alice in Wonderland.
Come follow us as we explore the magic
of traveling through the looking-glass,
attending the many tea parties that Alice herself,
both the character in the stories and the real little girl,
would have attended.

Welcome to Alice's Wonderland.

"Drink Me"

TEA WITH THE MAD HATTER

"Take some more tea," the March Hare said to Alice, very earnestly.

"I've had nothing yet," Alice replied in an offended tone: "so I can't take more."

"You mean you can't take *less*," said the Hatter: "it's very easy to take *more* than nothing."

—FROM "A MAD TEA PARTY"
ALICE'S ADVENTURES IN WONDERLAND

et's pretend. Two very simple words, really. But two that inspire imagination. Tea with the Mad Hatter is just such an occasion to turn a flight of fantasy into reality. The stage can be set so the very best of Wonderland can belong to each guest. As they gallantly line up to begin their Mad Hatter adventure, tiny bottles tied at the neck with DRINK ME tags await consumption by

each time they are instructed to take a bite of their own EAT ME cake, they will shrink or grow on command. In so doing, games and activities can be changed at the wink of an eye, or at the discretion of the host(ess).

In planning for this affair, a good imagination should be used to decide who, exactly, the Mad Hatter will be. Surely begin with the guest of honor, but the Mad Hatter can also be a fun-loving brother or father, entertaining aunt, or any good-

each little partygoer, assuring that something very special is going to happen today. As they take their places at the Mad Hatter's tea table, they will be told that

in any direction of fancy. Once they've properly placed their "mad hats" upon their heads and consumed enough treats from the tea menu, they'll be ready to play. When they are asked to take a bite of their EAT ME cake, imaginations take hold as they shrink to the size of the White Rabbit, and Looking-Glass Games such as

Menu

THE WHITE RABBIT'S
TEA SANDWICHES

THE MAD HATTER'S
PARTY PINWHEELS

"EAT ME" CAKES

THE CATERPILLAR'S
MUSHROOM MERINGUES

"DRINK ME" TEA

THE DORMOUSE'S
"TEAPOT" ICED TEA

natured person willing to take on the responsibility of directing the day's festivities. Not available? A life-sized doll can be fashioned to sit at a prominent place at the table. Or Mother can don the high hat and take charge. A special Mad Hatter voice can be prerecorded and played at intervals. Or, numbered "Hatter Notes" can be left in placecard envelopes at each seat, instructing each guest on what's to come.

As the tea begins, guests can be guided

Musical Toadstools or Pin On the Cheshire Grin can begin.

When it's time to grow larger than life, guests are sent back to the table for another bite of cake and their next instruction. Reaching-Through-the-House is an amusing way to give children the feeling of being "bigger than life—just like Alice" as they

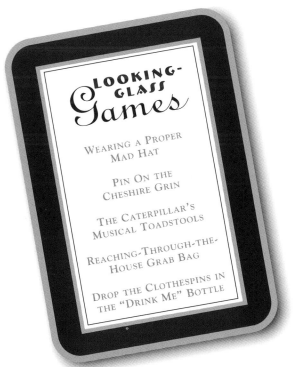

LOOKING-GLASS Games

WEARING A PROPER MAD HAT

PIN ON THE CHESHIRE GRIN

THE CATERPILLAR'S MUSICAL TOADSTOOLS

REACHING-THROUGH-THE-HOUSE GRAB BAG

DROP THE CLOTHESPINS IN THE "DRINK ME" BOTTLE

grab their gift through the windows of a dollhouse.

Table settings can be as whimsical as time and effort can afford. Use mismatched china and serveware, or use your everyday dishes and line them with beautiful paper doilies for a lovely presentation that's also easy to clean. If extra effort is made, even the smallest of details will not go unnoticed. White gloves can be carefully placed on the table and a "Pocket Watch" placecard can honor every plate. Faces will beam at the engaging "Caterpillar's Mushroom Meringues," and at the end of the table, a tiny stuffed dormouse can curl up to catch forty winks.

This tea party is unlike any other, and as Alice would say, "curiouser and curiouser." At this event, nothing is quite what it seems, yet everything is altogether totally delightful.

"DRINK ME"

5

Drink Me
R E C I P E S

The White Rabbit's Tea Sandwiches

....

BECAUSE THE WHITE RABBIT ENJOYS ALL TYPES OF
VEGETABLES, HIS TEA SANDWICHES ARE FILLED WITH A
VARIETY OF HIS GARDEN FAVORITES.

MAKES ABOUT 24 FINGER SANDWICHES
Dill-Mint Mayonnaise
> 1 cup mayonnaise
> ⅓ cup finely chopped fresh dill
> 2 Tbsp. fresh mint, finely minced

Mix all ingredients well. Keep refrigerated in
a covered container until ready to use.

Choose One of the Following Fillings
> 1 bunch watercress, stems removed
>
> 2 carrots, grated, and 2 Tbsp. raisins
>
> 2–3 chopped hard-cooked eggs, dash of salt
> and pepper; with 2–3 Tbsp. Dill-
> Mint Mayonnaise

Spread firm white bread with a light coating of
unsalted butter, then cut in triangles, or use
decorative cookie cutters in flower, heart, pocket watch, or bunny shapes. Spread shapes with
Dill-Mint Mayonnaise and one of the fillings.
Place damp tea towel over sandwiches if not
serving immediately.

The Mad Hatter's Party Pinwheels

....

ANY SMOOTH, CREAMY FILLING IS IDEAL FOR THESE
PINWHEEL SANDWICHES. YOU CAN CHOOSE FROM OUR
SELECTION OR USE YOUR OWN FAMILY FAVORITE—JUST
MAKE SURE IT'S SPREADABLE.

MAKES 12–18 PINWHEELS
Whipped Cream Cheese (1 8-oz. tub)
**Mixed with any one of the following, per
individual 8-oz. tub:**
- 3 Tbsp. finely chopped chives
- ⅓ cup mashed strawberries
- ¼ cup raisins and ½ tsp. cinnamon
- 1 grated apple and ½ tsp. cinnamon
- ⅓ cup fruit (such as canned peaches,
pears, tangerines, mandarin oranges, grapes,
or cherries)

Combine ingredients in the bowl of a food processor and process until smooth. Keep refrigerated in a covered container, then bring to room temperature when ready to use.

Pinwheel Sandwiches: To assemble, spread soft cracker bread with a layer of Whipped Cream Cheese Mixture, spreading enough to cover all but one 3" edge. Roll up so your sandwich roll ends with the empty edge, then wrap tightly in plastic wrap and refrigerate for at least 1 hour or longer. When ready to serve, slice ½" thick and serve immediately.

Raspberry Butter Pinwheels: Follow directions above, substituting Whipped Cream Cheese Mixture with Raspberry Butter.

Raspberry Butter
> 8 Tbsp. (1 stick) unsalted butter, softened
> 2 tsp. lemon juice
> 4–5 Tbsp. seedless raspberry jam

"Eat Me" Cakes

It's time for a visit to your favorite bakery! When ordering, explain to your baker that you would like a number (count your guests, then add 4) of small white, yellow, or chocolate cakes, all made in the same shape. Bring along a favorite cookie cutter for the baker to use, or have the cakes cut in diamond shapes before icing is poured over them. Iced like petits fours, these cakes should have the words EAT ME piped across the tops.

The Caterpillar's Mushroom Meringues

Many bakeries will make these for you—just give them a few days' notice. Recipes for these meringues are available in many of your favorite dessert cookbooks.

The Dormouse's "Teapot" Iced Tea

Because children appreciate any opportunity to have a *real* tea party, any of the teas mentioned on page 39 can be served as "Teapot" Iced Teas. Simply brew, refrigerate, and serve the tea in your favorite teapot—well chilled. Put ice cubes in teacups or small glasses and pour in your "Teapot" Iced Tea. The White Knight's Limeade and The Knave of Hearts' Tart Lemonade (see page 27) can also be served in this same way, and children love it.

Looking-Glass Games

WEARING A PROPER MAD HAT

When inviting guests to your "mad" tea party, make sure your invitation includes: "Please bring your 'maddest' hat." If someone forgets to bring one, make sure to have a few on hand. Make it a contest, where all guests can vote for who has the maddest hat of the tea party. The one who wins can be honorary Mad Hatter, who pours the tea or drinks for the duration of the afternoon. After all, this *is* a mad tea party!

PIN ON THE CHESHIRE GRIN

This game is very much like Pin the Tail on the Donkey. Find your favorite illustration of the Cheshire Cat (we like Tenniel's) and enlarge it several times on a copy machine, so the cat has a 4" x 6" grin. Make as many copies as there are guests. Hand-color one copy of the entire cat, leaving the grin and teeth uncolored. Cut out the grin from the rest of your copies, and give each child a grin to color, letting them print their name in the teeth. Then place a piece of double-stick tape on the back

of everyone's grin. Affix the Cheshire Cat to a tree, door, or wall. One at a time, line little guests up and blindfold with a scarf, spin them around three times, and let them find their way to the Cheshire Cat. Try not to let them feel their way around—start them out with an outstretched hand so they can affix the grin in only one place. Leave up all grins until the final child plays. The one whose grin has been placed closest to the real Cheshire grin wins.

THE CATERPILLAR'S MUSICAL TOADSTOOLS

Another fun variation of an age-old favorite is Musical Toadstools. For the sake of authenticity, have each guest bring a small step stool, ottoman, or footstool to the party. Start one "toadstool" short, placing them in a circle. Have all guests stand in front of the toadstools as you begin the music. Play it for 30 seconds or so, then stop the music. Have each child quickly sit on the nearest toadstool. He or she who is left standing leaves the game. Remove another toadstool, and continue to play until there are only two children and one toadstool remaining. The final toadstool sitter wins.

REACHING-THROUGH-THE-HOUSE GRAB BAG

Use your favorite dollhouse, or enlist a friend who has one with windows suitable for a small arm to reach through. If you're fortunate enough to have a playhouse in the yard with windows, this will also work well. All guests should be gathered around the inside of the dollhouse, where the rooms are. The host or hostess of the party should be on the outside of the house with the grab bag. One at a time, let your little guests reach through their window to obtain their grab bag gift.

DROP THE CLOTHESPINS IN THE "DRINK ME" BOTTLE

This game of skill is ideal for children ages eight and up. You'll need a glass milk bottle and six wooden clothespins. Tie the neck of the milk bottle with a large DRINK ME tag and place on the ground. Have guests line up and hand the first in line the six clothespins. Have them stand over the bottle and drop them in. The youngster able to drop in the most clothespins wins.

Please bring your "maddest" hat

PAINTING
the Roses Red

❦

TEA IN THE GARDEN

"Would you tell me, please," said Alice, a little timidly, "why you are painting those roses?" Five and Seven said nothing, but looked at Two. Two began, in a low voice, "Why, the fact is, you see, Miss, this here ought to have been a red rose-tree, and we put a white one in by mistake; and, if the Queen was to find out, we should all have our heads cut off, you know. So you see, Miss, we're doing our best ..."

—FROM "THE QUEEN'S CROQUET GROUND"
ALICE'S ADVENTURES IN WONDERLAND

*a*nd so begins the infamous Wonderland scene, in which the Queen gives a command that the royal garden's roses be red, thus forcing her three gardeners to dash madly about, painting her *white* roses *red*, or surely lose their heads. For your tea in the garden, blooming roses are the flower of choice, but are far from obligatory. This distinguished event should take place

when perennial gardens are in full bloom, hedgerows are densely packed, and the lawn is thick and green.

Invitations are written by the Queen of Hearts herself, and in her own noble fashion, Her Royal Highness imposes rules before any guest can accept the

Queen's invitation:

Each Guest who attends My Tea must be dedicated to Having Fun throughout this Topsy-Turvy Day. Furthermore, Each Guest must be willing to play New Games in a Way That They may have Never Played Them before.

To begin, inform each child that throughout the day, he or she will have a turn at being the Queen of Hearts, bellowing out commands to other party guests during the playing of Looking-Glass Games. A good icebreaker is Guess the Royal Guest, where each attendee has an "Alice" character written on paper and attached to their back, and they must ask questions of one another to determine who their character is. Musical Chairs is transformed into a round of "Off with Their Heads," where unfortunate chair seekers turn the tables and shout "Off with his [or her] head!" when the next participant is caught short of a chair. Soon, the entire crowd chimes in, until the last of the group is declared the winner—and is rewarded with the ability to hold on to his or her head.

Because this tea takes place on the Queen's Croquet Ground, what better game to play than Flamingo Croquet? If you cannot get your pink flamingos to cooperate as Alice did, perhaps you can invite them to be present,

Menu

ROYAL FINGER SANDWICHES

THE QUEEN'S CREAM SCONES

COEURS À LA CRÈME WITH STRAWBERRIES

LEMON-RASPBERRY LOOKING-GLASS CAKE

THE WHITE KNIGHT'S LIMEADE

ALICE'S RASPBERRY ROYALTEA

keeping watch over each player and standing guard by key wickets. The Painting-the-Roses-Red Relay will allow each guest to run off some of their energy, running back and forth, filling all white rose bushes until they are blushing bright red.

To dress your table for the royal occasion, use a red rose tablecloth, or use a plain tablecloth scattered with bright red rose petals. Ruby red plates or clear glass luncheon sets are ideal; simply let your teatime edibles garnished with fresh mint and berries do the decorating for you.

The foods chosen are true to the theme of the tea, and are as delicious as they are suitable for any out-of-doors affair. Royal Finger Sandwiches are shaped like diamonds, the Queen's Cream Scones are a favorite with a "clotted" cream and fresh fruit jam, and petite heart shaped Coeurs à la Crème with Strawberries are a luscious accompaniment to any warm-weather occa-

LOOKING-GLASS Games

GUESS THE ROYAL GUEST

"OFF WITH THEIR HEADS" MUSICAL CHAIRS

PAINTING-THE-ROSES-RED RELAY

FLAMINGO CROQUET

THE QUEEN OF HEARTS' TREASURE CHEST

sion. The food culminates with the beautiful and delicious Lemon-Raspberry Looking-Glass Cake, pretty as a picture and simply adorned with lemon leaves, orange blossoms, and fresh raspberries. Just before guests depart, end the day with a trip to The Queen of Hearts' Treasure Chest, a golden opportunity to reward loyal subjects.

PAINTING the Roses Red RECIPES

The Queen's Cream Scones

FIT FOR A QUEEN ON HER SPECIAL DAY, OR FOR ANYONE
DESERVING OF THE ROYAL TREATMENT. SERVE WARM WITH
FRUIT JAM AND "CLOTTED" CREAM (PAGE 62).

MAKES 10 SCONES

2 cups all-purpose flour
¼ cup granulated sugar
1 Tbsp. baking powder
1 tsp. salt
4 Tbsp. (½ stick) cold unsalted butter
1 large egg
1¼ cups heavy cream
Additional cream for brushing

Preheat oven to 350°F. Lightly grease a baking
sheet; set aside. In a medium bowl, sift together
dry ingredients. Cut in butter with a pastry
cutter or 2 knives until mixture is the texture
of cornmeal. In a small bowl, combine egg and
cream. Pour into dry ingredients and mix
until blended. The dough will be slightly wet.
Turn dough out onto a well-floured surface
and pat dough to ¾" thickness. Cut out scones
with 2½" biscuit cutter and place on baking
sheet. Brush tops with additional heavy
cream. Bake 25 minutes, or until golden
brown.

For Petal Scones: Cut with flower-shaped
cookie cutter.

Coeurs à la Crème with Strawberries

THIS CREAMY, LIGHT MOUSSELIKE DESSERT MAKES 8
SMALL OR 1 LARGE HEART-SHAPED DESSERT. BE SURE TO
BEGIN AT LEAST 1 DAY AHEAD OF YOUR PARTY, AS THIS
MUST SET OVERNIGHT BEFORE SERVING.

SERVES 8

1 cup ricotta cheese
2 Tbsp. superfine sugar
1 tsp. fresh lemon juice
2 large egg whites
1¼ cups whipping cream
Fresh mint and pansies for garnish
1–2 pints fresh strawberries

Press ricotta through a sieve into a bowl. Mix in sugar and lemon juice; set aside. In another bowl, beat egg whites until stiff peaks form. Fold egg whites into cheese mixture. Whip cream until stiff; add to cheese mixture. Line 8 small heart-shaped molds (openweave baskets or molds with drainage holes) or 1 large mold with cheesecloth. Spoon in cheese mixture. Place on a plate and refrigerate overnight to drain. To serve, unmold onto a serving plate, then gently remove cheesecloth. Garnish with mint and pansies. Serve with fresh strawberries.

Lemon-Raspberry Looking-Glass Cake

THE CROWNING GLORY TO YOUR MAJESTIC EVENT, THIS LUSCIOUS THREE-LAYER CAKE IS AN ALL-TIME FAVORITE AT THE SWEET LADY JANE TEAROOM.

SERVES 12

Raspberry Filling
1½ pints (2¼ cups) fresh raspberries
¼ cup granulated sugar
2 Tbsp. unsalted butter
1 Tbsp. fresh lemon juice
1 Tbsp. cornstarch
2 large egg yolks

Lemon Curd
½ cup fresh lemon juice
½ cup granulated sugar
2 Tbsp. unsalted butter
1 large egg
1 large egg yolk

Cake
3 cups sifted all-purpose flour
4 tsp. baking powder
¾ tsp. salt
3 large eggs
1 cup milk
2 tsp. vanilla
12 Tbsp. (1½ sticks) unsalted butter, softened
1⅔ cups granulated sugar

Lemon Cream Frosting
1 cup (2 sticks) unsalted butter, softened
4 cups confectioners' sugar
3 Tbsp. fresh lemon juice

Raspberry Filling
In a small saucepan, combine raspberries, sugar, butter, and lemon juice. Cook, stirring constantly, over medium-low heat until berries are very soft and lose their shape. Press raspberry mixture through a sieve, discarding seeds and pulp. Measure 1 cup puree. Cool. In same saucepan, mix cornstarch and 2 Tbsp. puree until smooth; set aside. In a small bowl, whisk egg yolks, then gradually whisk in remaining raspberry puree. Add to cornstarch mixture in saucepan, and place over medium-high heat. Begin whisking in saucepan and cook, stirring constantly, until mixture thickens slightly and almost boils. Pour into a bowl and press plastic wrap directly onto surface of filling. Cool to room temperature, about 2 hours, then refrigerate until cold, another 2 hours. Can be prepared up to 3 days ahead of time.   (cont'd)

Lemon Curd

In another small saucepan, combine lemon juice, sugar, and butter. Cook, stirring constantly, over medium-low heat until sugar dissolves and butter melts. Cool. In a medium bowl, whisk together egg and egg yolk. Gradually whisk in cooled lemon mixture. Return to saucepan. Cook, stirring constantly, over medium-low heat until mixture thickens slightly and almost boils. Pour into bowl. Press plastic wrap directly onto surface of filling. Cool to room temperature, about 2 hours. Refrigerate until cold, about 2 hours. Can be prepared up to 3 days ahead of time.

Cake

Preheat oven to 350°F. Butter and flour 3 (9" x 1½") layer-cake pans. Line bottoms with wax paper. Butter and flour paper. Sift together flour, baking powder, and salt; set aside. In a medium bowl, whisk together eggs, milk, and vanilla; set aside. In a large mixing bowl, beat butter with an electric mixer on high until light and creamy. Gradually beat in sugar, beating until light and fluffy, scraping sides of bowl often. Add flour mixture alternately with milk mixture, beginning and ending with flour mixture, beating until smooth after each addition. Beat for 1 minute; divide batter between pans. Bake 25 minutes until wooden toothpick comes out clean. Cool in pans set on racks 10 minutes, then cover pans with racks and invert. Peel off wax paper. Cool on racks.

Lemon Cream Frosting

In large mixing bowl, beat butter with electric mixer at medium speed until light and creamy. Gradually add confectioners' sugar, beating well after each addition and scraping sides of bowl often. Slowly add lemon juice, beating until smooth.

To Assemble

Just before serving, arrange 1 cake layer on serving plate. Spread top with lemon curd. Top with another cake layer. Spread top with raspberry filling. Arrange last cake layer on top. Reserve 1 cup frosting. Spread top and sides of cake with remaining frosting. Using the star tip of a pastry tube, pipe reserved frosting decoratively on cake. Refrigerate any leftover cake.

Looking-Glass Games

PAINTING-THE-ROSES-RED RELAY

Rather than using actual thorny rosebushes, use two nice green hedges instead. Before the party begins, stick white silk roses all over both hedges (not too high!), making sure you will have at least two white roses per player. Line the children up in two lines for the relay, giving them each a red silk rose. The object of the game is to run to the "rosebush," remove one white rose, and replace it with one red rose. Each youngster will have two chances to run the relay, so make sure someone is there at both sides of the line to hand them their second red rose. Time the relay with the second hand of a watch. (A pocket watch would be authentic for the official White Rabbit timekeeper!) Time the relay to be age-appropriate for your guests—the younger, the longer. At the end of the designated time, the team with the most red roses in their rosebush wins.

FLAMINGO CROQUET

Because real flamingos refuse to cooperate like they did for Alice, you'll need a wooden croquet set and several plastic pink flamingos. Set up the croquet set and place a pink flamingo near several "key" wickets. The person who hits the croquet ball through these "flamingo wickets" with the least number of strokes wins.

The Queen of Hearts' Treasure Chest

To reward little guests for attending and participating and to make sure no one goes home empty-handed, tiny gifts, *all exactly the same*, are included in the Queen of Hearts' Treasure Chest. Make sure you make a few extra for unexpected little brothers and sisters who may appear.

THE CORONATION
OF
Queen Alice

A NURSERY TEA

"Then fill up the glasses with treacle and ink, Or anything else that is
pleasant to drink: Mix sand with the cider, and wool with the wine—
And welcome Queen Alice with ninety-times-nine!"

—FROM "QUEEN ALICE"
THROUGH THE LOOKING GLASS

This chapter is for those that are customarily the very best at imaginary tea parties: the youngest, smallest, and dearest. The Coronation of Queen Alice is a wonderful opportunity for little ones to take part in their very own real-life tea party, which will probably be their first. Invite only the most intimate of playmates, taking care that your total number of tiny guests does not exceed

to help with the party activities, and the parents can take advantage of one of the most precious photo opportunities ever.

Pull out the stops for this special occasion. Not only is this the beginning of your child's formal introduction to taking tea, it is a coronation, after all! This event could commemorate a third or fourth birthday, or officially celebrate the commencement of the warm days of spring. When you reflect on it, perhaps the only reason you really need is your heartfelt commitment to give your child a very happy, joyful day.

Once the children arrive for their special Coronation Tea, each will have the opportunity to be Queen Alice, or in the case of masculine guests, Kings or White

the age of your child (an excellent party rule for parents with children under the age of twelve). In addition to Coronation Tea guests, it is also a wonderful idea to invite as many parents as would like to attend. This provides the perfect chance for you to have a few voluntary assistants

Knights. Invitations can be fashioned like crowns, with all vital party information written on the inside of the crown. If desired, each can wear their respective crowns at the table, or a special "Queen Alice" crown can be made of stronger materials, bejeweled for a finishing touch. To complete this majestic event, have a special imperial scepter and royal robe on hand so that each guest can take a turn leading the Coronation Parade of Queen Alice and Her Loyal Subjects. This procession

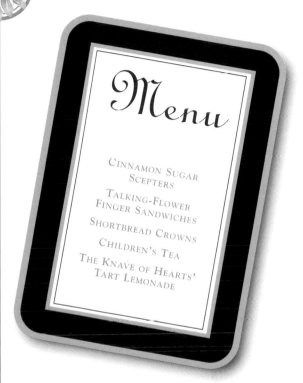

Menu

CINNAMON SUGAR
SCEPTERS

TALKING-FLOWER
FINGER SANDWICHES

SHORTBREAD CROWNS

CHILDREN'S TEA

THE KNAVE OF HEARTS'
TART LEMONADE

guides the guests of the royal court to their first teatime celebration.

At the tea table, take heed that the linens used can withstand the rigor of splashes and spills, and that the dishes are of the industrial-strength variety to accommodate lilliputian hands of Herculean strength. Appoint an espe-

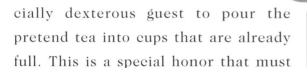

cially dexterous guest to pour the pretend tea into cups that are already full. This is a special honor that must not be taken lightly, for the pouring of the pretend tea is what creates the magic in every guest's cup. Those who

drink of the magic are granted the gift of good manners, and these guests will be forever blessed with invitations to many tea parties to come.

Little ones love to play at lots of different activities within a very short time, so Looking-Glass nursery games are fun and easy enough for just about any child to perform. Play music or have a younger child pound out a rhythm on a drum for Pass the Scepter, a game much like Hot Potato with a royal twist. Duck...Duck...Dodo! is fun once children have enjoyed their teatime treats, but reserve this game for children who are at least four years of age, as excitement tends to ensue during the obligatory light-tap-on-the-head stage of the game.

For a special treat just before small guests depart, send them on Alice's Golden Egg Hunt, which allows them to search for and retrieve one (or two)

of their own party favors. Provide two Golden Eggs per guest, allowing for one egg to be cracked at party time, revealing a special surprise inside, and the other to be brought home as a precious memento of the day's most sovereign festivities.

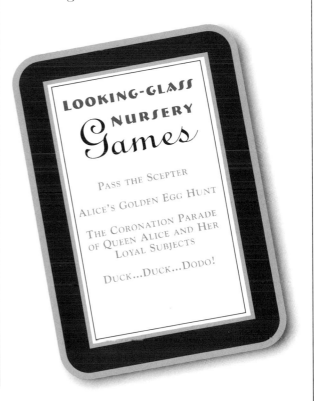

LOOKING-GLASS NURSERY Games

PASS THE SCEPTER

ALICE'S GOLDEN EGG HUNT

THE CORONATION PARADE OF QUEEN ALICE AND HER LOYAL SUBJECTS

DUCK...DUCK...DODO!

RECIPES
The Coronation of Queen Alice

Cinnamon Sugar Scepters

THESE PUFF PASTRY SCEPTERS ARE EASY TO MAKE, KEEP WELL, AND CHILDREN LOVE THEM.

MAKES ABOUT 12–18 SCEPTERS

1 package frozen puff pastry, cool but not quite thawed
Cinnamon
Granulated sugar

Preheat oven to 350°F. Line a baking sheet with parchment paper. Roll out puff pastry dough into a rectangle, approximately 18" x 20". Sprinkle with cinnamon and sugar, then gently press mixture into dough with rolling pin. Fold dough in half crosswise, then roll out again to 18" x 20". Sprinkle evenly with cinnamon and sugar. Cut in 1" strips. Twist each strip into a corkscrew and place closely side by side on parchment-covered baking sheet. Bake until puffed and brown, about 18 minutes. Remove from oven; let rest 10 minutes, then cut apart if necessary. Finish cooling on racks. Store in plastic bags until ready to use. Will keep at room temperature for 3–4 days.

Talking-Flower Finger Sandwiches

Use your favorite flower-shaped cookie cutter to create these lovely little sandwiches. Cut out bread slices first, then spread with your child's favorite filling. A flower-shaped slice of cheese in the middle adds a nice surprise!

Shortbread Crowns

THE LIDDELL FAMILY RECIPE FOR SCOTCH SHORTBREAD WAS BROUGHT TO THE UNITED STATES FROM ENGLAND BY GEORGE TURNER LIDDELL II'S GRANDMOTHER, ESTHER STEWART LIDDELL. WHEN GEORGE MAKES SHORTBREAD, HE DOUBLES THE SUGAR AND REDUCES THE FLOUR BY ½ CUP. HERE IS THE ORIGINAL FOR YOU TO DECIDE.

MAKES 12 CROWNS
> ½ lb. butter
> 4 T. sugar
> 3 "small" cups flour

Preheat oven to 275°F. Cream butter with sugar. Add flour, a little at a time, beating carefully. Add more flour until it can be handled without sticking. Make into a ball, pinch portions off, flatten with hands, and pinch edges between thumb and finger.

For Shortbread Crowns, lightly roll out until ½" thick and cut with crown cookie cutter. Place crowns on baking sheet. Bake until slightly brown, approximately 25–35 minutes.

For Shortbread Wheel, flatten dough into an ungreased pie plate or quiche pan and score the top to make it easy to break into pieces when cooked. Prick surface with fork and bake slowly at moderate heat until slightly brown, 45 minutes–1 hour.

The Knave of Hearts' Tart Lemonade

FOR THOSE LONG, HOT DAYS OF SUMMER, NOTHING REFRESHES BETTER THAN A COLD GLASS OF LEMONADE OVER ICE.

SERVES 12
> 6 lemons, scrubbed
> 2 cups granulated sugar
> 1 cup water
> Dash of salt

Using a citrus zester, carefully zest 2 lemons and chop zest coarsely. Place zest, sugar, water, and salt in a saucepan. Cover with lid and boil 5 minutes. Remove from heat and let cool. Juice all 6 lemons and add juice to syrup. Strain. When ready to serve, use 2–4 Tbsp. lemonade syrup to 1 glass ice water or lemon-flavored sparkling water. Syrup will keep in the refrigerator for about 1 week, or freeze indefinitely.

Looking-Glass Nursery Games

PASS THE SCEPTER

If you need to fashion a scepter, glue a wooden knob or Styrofoam ball to a wooden dowel, spray-paint with gold paint, adorn as desired with "jewels" (you can hot-glue them to the ball on top), and tie with a flowing scarf. To play Pass the Scepter, have little guests stand in a circle, handing one person the scepter. The object is to quickly pass (not throw) the scepter to the person next to you, so you are not left with it in your hand. The host or hostess plays the music as the scepter is passed. When the music stops, he or she who is left holding the scepter is out. The last person left empty-handed wins.

ALICE'S GOLDEN EGG HUNT

A few days before party time, take one dozen eggs (or at least two per guest) and with a pushpin, prick the shell at both ends of

the egg. Using the pushpin to chip away some of the shell on one end (open up to about ½"), blow the egg from the small end out the large end. Separate out at least one egg white and reserve. Leave empty eggs, large-hole side down, to finish draining in the carton. When dry, fill each egg with confetti, then place a small piece of white tissue paper over the large open end. Paint with egg white to affix tissue paper. Let dry in egg carton, then spray-paint metallic gold. Hide eggs all around the garden, and let your guests search for 2 each. What a surprise they'll get when they break them to find a rainbow of confetti inside!

THE CORONATION PARADE OF
Queen Alice
AND HER LOYAL SUBJECTS

To satisfy every guest's desire to wear the crown and carry the scepter, let each one take a turn. A royal robe can be made from any scarf tied at the neck and lightly draped over the shoulders. Play a royal march as the children parade around the grounds, the Queen or King at the front of the line holding the scepter high as the robe floats in the wind and loyal subjects follow. This is a photo opportunity no parent should miss.

DUCK...DUCK...DODO!

Gather all guests into a circle and sit them down. Have one person be It, who gently taps each person on the head as he/she walks around the circle saying "Duck," "Duck," "Duck." When arriving at the person he/she chooses to be the next It, he/she taps that person on the head and says "Dodo!" They take off running to find the next available place to sit down in the circle. If the person who is the new It cannot touch the person who was It before he/she sits down, then that person remains It and starts the game again. Ideal for ages four and up.

IN HONOR OF
Saint Valentine

❦

CUPID'S TEA

LOVE'S GREETING

This is the greeting of a friend,
For more than that I dare not send;
But let me whisper to you, dear,

I hope before another year,
That you'll to me your heart incline
And take me for your Valentine.

—FROM MY HEART IS THINE,
VICTORIAN VALENTINE

Our Cupid's Tea is a tea party with a purpose: to re-create the fun-loving and industrious activity of the lost art of crafting valentines. It was Victorian custom to gather friends together in advance of Saint Valentine's Day so all could earnestly design valentines for family and friends. Because this tradition is genuinely female, have all the girls dress in their finest teatime

attire, and have them accompanied by their favorite doll. If you have a small table, cloak it with a piano scarf for a tablecloth, a tiny tea set, and miniature dishes filled with tiny scones and small candies from which the dolls can enjoy a Cupid's Tea of their own. This is also a wonderful opportunity for you to take a

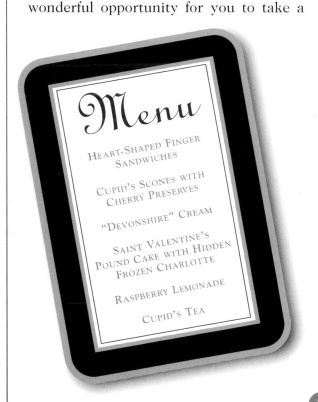

Menu

HEART-SHAPED FINGER
SANDWICHES

CUPID'S SCONES WITH
CHERRY PRESERVES

"DEVONSHIRE" CREAM

SAINT VALENTINE'S
POUND CAKE WITH HIDDEN
FROZEN CHARLOTTE

RASPBERRY LEMONADE

CUPID'S TEA

picture of each of your guests, doll at her side as her guest of honor on this very special day.

To facilitate ease of transition between valentine making and the taking of tea, separate tables should be set up for each. Set your Valentine tea table with luxurious red roses and tulips, fresh grapes, and all teatime edibles, buffet style. This way, each guest can help herself to a variety of sandwiches, scones, and other treats.

The Saint Valentine's Pound Cake

hides a special surprise, and her name is Frozen Charlotte. The German legend of Frozen Charlotte and Frozen Charlie dates back more than one hundred years, a sad story of young love forever lost to vanity. To commemorate the tale of the young lovers and to forever capture their memory, mid-nineteenth-century craftsmen designed porcelain figures in different sizes, many of which are still available in antique shops throughout the world. This small porcelain doll was traditionally baked inside Victorian cakes. The lucky one who finds Charlotte (or Charlie) in her piece of cake is assured to find true love forever! Once the cake has been cut, enjoyed, and Frozen Charlotte found, it's time for the lost art of craft-

ing valentines.

To make the valentines, lots of preparation must go into the gathering of the various papers, the cutting of shapes, doilies, bits of lace, trim, bric-a-brac, ribbon, rubber stamps, and Victorian stickers, along with enough construction

will be awarded a special certificate for her creative efforts. If you wish, accompany the certificate of honor with a little gift for each guest, for crafting the best valentines their sweethearts will ever have the pleasure of receiving. Before you bid your guests a fond adieu, make sure each has made her own "Big-Hearted" envelope in which to carry home the treasures of the heart.

paper to fashion the base of each valentine creation. Take a look in old books for Victorian valentine quotes and pen them for your young participants, assisting them in creating a true Victorian classic, and helping embellish upon their feelings for the upcoming 14th of February, "Love's Own Day."

To give credit where it is due, create a special ceremony called a "Valentine Honorarium" where each valentine crafter

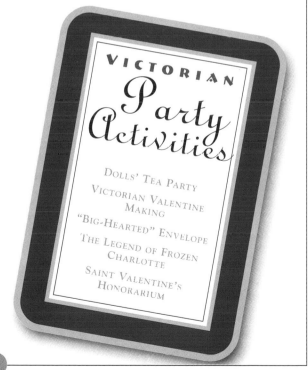

VICTORIAN
Party
Activities

DOLLS' TEA PARTY

VICTORIAN VALENTINE MAKING

"BIG-HEARTED" ENVELOPE

THE LEGEND OF FROZEN CHARLOTTE

SAINT VALENTINE'S HONORARIUM

RECIPES
In Honor of
Saint Valentine

How to Prepare Finger Sandwiches

Breads: Use a loaf of thinly sliced firm white or wheat bread, preferably from your bakery. For color and variety, use jalapeño-cheese, dark squaw, cinnamon-raisin, or whole-grain breads. However, these alternates have a more robust taste, so make sure your filling can stand up to the strong flavor of the bread.

To Prepare Sandwiches: When you're ready to begin, dampen a tea towel and keep the bread you're using completely covered. Cut with a cookie cutter into shapes, or cut with a sharp knife and remove crusts and cut into squares, triangles, or rectangles and stack in manageable, even-numbered stacks. Return stacks to the tea towel. Just before party time, spread with filling. Keep covered with damp tea towel in the refrigerator approximately ½ hour, until ready to serve.

Filling Suggestions: When preparing finger sandwiches, choose two savory and one sweet filling to serve your guests. There are many easy, delightful fillings you can add to basic ingredients. These are some of our favorites, but use your imagination while considering the tastes of your little guests (see also page 6).

Whipped Cream Cheese Thinly Spread On Bread and Topped with:
- 2 tsp. crispy bacon, crumbled (simple, but always a favorite)
- A thin slice of smoked salmon and a sprig of fresh dill
- 2–3 paper-thin slices of English cucumber, drained in paper toweling, sprinkled with white pepper

Sweet Butter Thinly Spread On Bread and Topped with:

- 5–6 paper-thin slices of radish and topped with a sprig of watercress
- 1 Tbsp. mashed avocado mixed with ½ tsp. finely chopped walnuts and topped with alfalfa sprouts (excellent on squaw bread)

Your Favorite Sandwich Salad Fillings, Finely Chopped and Thinly Spread On Bread:

- ½ lb. egg salad mixed with 1 Tbsp. fresh dill
- ½ lb. chicken salad mixed with 2 Tbsp. mango chutney
- ½ lb. ham salad mixed with 1 small, finely chopped apple

Cupid's Scones with Cherry Preserves

TO PROPERLY HONOR SAINT VALENTINE, LITTLE CUPIDS ENJOY HEART-SHAPED SCONES TOPPED WITH SPARKLING SUGAR CRYSTALS AND SERVED WITH "DEVONSHIRE" CREAM (PAGE 62) AND CHERRY PRESERVES.

MAKES 12–16 HEART-SHAPED SCONES

4 cups unsifted all-purpose flour
¼ cup granulated sugar
1 Tbsp. baking powder
½ tsp. salt
½ tsp. baking soda
⅔ cup (1 stick + 3 Tbsp.) unsalted butter
1½ cups buttermilk
Sugar crystals (rainbow-colored or red), for garnish
"Devonshire" Cream and cherry preserves, for serving

Preheat oven to 425°F. Line a baking sheet with parchment paper, or grease well. Combine dry ingredients. Cut in butter with pastry cutter or 2 knives until mixture is the texture of cornmeal. Add buttermilk and mix until a soft dough forms. Knead dough on a lightly floured board until it holds its shape, being careful not to overhandle dough. Roll out to ½" thickness and cut with 2½" heart-shaped cutter. Place on baking sheet and sprinkle with sugar crystals. Bake 15 minutes, or until golden brown. Serve warm with "Devonshire" Cream (see page 62) and cherry preserves.

Saint Valentine's Pound Cake with Hidden Frozen Charlotte

THIS CAKE IS BEST WHEN MADE 1 DAY AHEAD.

SERVES 10-12

½ pint whipping cream
½ lb. (2 sticks) unsalted butter
3 cups granulated sugar
6 large eggs
3 cups sifted all-purpose flour
1 Tbsp. vanilla extract
(All ingredients should be at room temperature)

If you're lucky enough to have a porcelain Charlotte or Charlie, freeze overnight. Preheat oven to 325°F. Grease and flour a Bundt pan. Whip cream in a small bowl and set aside. Cream together butter and sugar until light and fluffy. Add eggs, 1 at a time. Fold in flour, vanilla, and whipped cream. Pour mixture into prepared Bundt pan. Drop frozen porcelain figure into batter. Bake 15 minutes, then reduce heat to 300°F and bake for 1¼ hours. Cake is done when cake tester comes out dry. Place Bundt pan on rack 20 minutes to set, then cover pan with rack and invert. Cool completely and wrap with plastic wrap. Store overnight in refrigerator. Slice carefully, minding little Charlotte or Charlie!

Whoever finds Frozen Charlotte or Charlie will find true love forever!

Raspberry Lemonade

Follow the recipe for The Knave of Hearts' Tart Lemonade (page 27). Puree 1 pint fresh raspberries or 1 frozen container raspberries; add to lemonade just before serving. Adjust sugar to taste.

The Perfect Pot of Tea

First, select a china teapot in which to brew and serve your tea. Tea should never be made in a teacup, as the leaves cannot steep properly. Begin by always using fresh water; if you are using water out of the tap, let it run a bit to aerate. Fill your teakettle with water and bring it to a full, rolling boil. While waiting for the water to boil, heat your teapot by pouring in hot water. Empty the water and add 1 tsp. tea leaves per cup of tea, then add 1 more for the pot. Once the water is boiling, for the hottest water possible, bring the pot to the kettle, and pour the boiling water over the tea leaves. Stir well and immediately put the top on so that the steam cannot escape. Allow the tea to steep for 5 minutes and serve. When you're ready for another pot, make sure to use new leaves. Loose tea leaves left in the pot for more than 5 minutes will begin to "stew," and will give your next pot a harsh, acidic flavor.

Our Favorite Teas

CHOOSE YOUR FAVORITE CAFFEINE-FREE HERBAL TEA, BREWING IT SOMEWHAT WEAK TO PLEASE THE UNINITIATED. BE SURE TO HAVE PLENTY OF MILK, SUGAR, AND LEMON SLICES AVAILABLE ON YOUR TEA TRAY.

"Drink Me" Tea
  Cranberry—delicious and refreshing
Alice's Raspberry Royaltea
  Raspberry—crisp and very raspberry
Children's Tea
  Strawberry Kiwi—fruity and fun
Cupid's Tea
  Country Peach—smooth and tangy
Fairy Tea
  Wild Berry—rich and deliciously berry (can also be brewed as a strong iced tea; serve well chilled with a sparkling water)
Saint Nicholas Tea
  Cinnamon Orange Spice—sweet and spicy
Other favorites
  Orange Mango—citrusy with a clean, fresh flavor
  Fruit and Almond—a favorite among the young at heart
  Jasmine—light and perfumed (brew quickly; it takes on a bitter flavor if brewed too long)
  Earl Grey—bergamot-scented for the adults
  Peppermint—minty and refreshing

Victorian Party Activities

VICTORIAN VALENTINE MAKING

There are few activities more industrious, imaginative, and thoughtful for your guests than creating their own Victorian valentines. An abundance of beautiful fabrics, laces, doilies, and French ribbons are available, as are handmade and hand-colored papers, and of course the standby, construction paper. Visit your favorite stationer for wrapping papers, gift tags, Victorian stickers, rubber stamps, and stamp pads in every color of the rainbow. Walk up and down the aisles of your local craft store; you'll find beautiful tiny silk flower embellishments in the wedding aisle, doilies of every shape and color in the cake-decorating aisle, and in the craft section, pastel hues of the finest glitter, ideal for Cupid's big day. Glue sticks are a necessity, along with scissors, pinking shears, and plenty of crayons and markers.

The appropriate sentiment is also an essential requirement for the valentine crafter, so dream up some of your own, or consult Victorian prose for authentic verbiage. When the big day finally arrives, place all craft items out where little hands can reach them, and assist younger ones with premade heart templates made from doilies or construction paper. Collect these items a little at a time throughout the year and keep them in a special "In Honor of Saint Valentine" box. When the 7th of February arrives, you'll be ready to craft the most beautiful valentines fit for any Victorian!

"BIG-HEARTED" ENVELOPE

Don't forget to have your guests make a large construction-paper envelope in a heart shape. Simply make two large, identical hearts, and staple or glue the bottom of each together, *right sides out*, leaving at least 3" unglued at the top of each side to allow for the easy insertion of the valentines. To make a handle, cut one 2" x 12" strip out of any left-over construction paper. Once valentines have been inserted, loop the handle and staple it to the top of each side of the envelope, being careful not to staple it shut! This "big-hearted" envelope will allow your guests to easily transport their handmade treasures home.

Saint Valentine's Honorarium

A fun way to end the party and reward your guests for their grandiose effort is to honor them with an award from Saint Valentine's Honorarium. These special awards (one for every child participating) are bestowed upon your valentine crafters for the following expertise: Most Beautiful, Most Colorful, Most Creative, Sweetest, Most Difficult, or Most Unusual. An ideal award is a little book of Victorian stickers or a Cupid rubber stamp, along with their own Saint Valentine's Honorarium Certificate, inscribed with their name and the name of the category in which their valentine placed. If you're creative, these certificates can be premade on the computer with the category already included. When awarding, simply write in the honoree's name. Tie the certificates with a grosgrain or French silk ribbon, and watch eyes light up when guests are handed such a special honor.

A Midsummer
NIGHT

TEA WITH THE FAIRIES

In the meadow—what is in the meadow?
Bluebells, buttercups, meadow sweet,
and fairy rings for children's feet.
In the meadow.

—CHRISTINA ROSSETTI (1830–1894)

Midsummer's Eve, traditionally celebrated on the evening of the 23rd of June, marks the halfway point of the year and is directly linked to the summer solstice. Rejoicing in the abundance and mystery of Nature, the Victorians gathered special flowers and herbs, which were believed to ward off the attentions of mischievous spirits and bless their gardens with noc-

quietly arrive as they do, on the wings of fireflies.

It's a very special honor to be invited to a Tea with the Fairies, for only those who truly believe will be blessed with the rewards of their presence. Multitudes of blooming flowers, visiting birds, dragonflies, ladybugs, butterflies, and a variety of other fairy rewards are in store for guests who sincerely believe and act accordingly. The party should commence in the late afternoon, at a timely hour for fairy activities to be completed by nightfall. To

turnal visits from friendly fairies. Our Midsummer Night Tea with the Fairies is just such an occasion, to honor the tiny winged friends with splendid foods, wee gardens, and fairy-favorable activities that will enchant the elfin population to

begin, all foods on the menu are favorites of the fairies, so you may pick and choose as many as you wish. However, remember, fairies *love* cake—itsy-bitsy tiny cakes, to be exact. Flight-of-Fancy Fairy Cakes are perfect, satisfying even the most reluctant of fairy visitors. To drink to the fairies' health, thimbles can be filled with Fairy Tea or lemonade and the toast

Menu

LEMON-BLUEBERRY
BUTTERFLY BITES

FAIRIES' FAVORITE FINGER
SANDWICHES

PETAL SCONES WITH
"DEVONSHIRE" CREAM AND
ENCHANTED VIOLET JELLY

FLIGHT-OF-FANCY
FAIRY CAKES

FAIRY RING

MIDSUMMER FAIRY PUNCH
WITH FROZEN FLOWER WREATH

FAIRY TEA

made:

O fairy sweet, on dewy wings—fly into
our garden, to you we greet!

Once the proper fairy-appropriate repast has been served, it's time to get down to business—fairy activities. First, a Fairy Garden can be planted or a flower Tussie-Mussie can be made right at the

VICTORIAN
Party Activities

MAKING A DAISY CHAIN
MAKING A FAIRY BED
PLANTING A FAIRY GARDEN
BLESSED WITH A FAIRY REWARD
THE LEGEND OF THE WITCHES' BALL

table. Because fairies tend to visit certain plants, it's important to have plenty of primroses, pansies, Johnny-jump-ups, shamrocks, thyme, and small ferns on hand. Once the planting is done, moss and lichens can be tucked around the plants, creating a fairy carpet. A Fairy Bed can be made with a walnut half, a

pussy willow for a pillow, and a fuzzy leaf for a tiny blanket. Guests can take home their Fairy Gardens or Tussie-Mussies, but must leave the Fairy Beds in a special place in the garden before they leave. In fact, fairies are known to hide under toadstools (or a Fairy Ring made from Mushroom Meringues), so if you find a few, place the beds nearby.

The Victorians believed that if fairy gardens were faithfully planted, as a reward for hospitality and goodness, gardens literally came alive. In fact, it is believed that fairies were at one time responsible for drawing the faces on Johnny-jump-ups, and upon close inspection, the center of the flower reveals a "bewhiskered kitty face."

What is so inspiring about such a tea party is that it is so much fun for those that are unfamiliar with the wisdom of believing in fairies, and for those who already believe, so rewarding. Something magic happens to those who speak in hushed tones of the flying twilight visitors, those who keep the valued secrets, yet continue to share the fairy lore with younger generations.

Listen carefully and keep a close

lookout for fairy friends. Once you witness them, the magic starts from within, and radiates out to the garden they walk through, and the flowers they speak to, as rays of sunshine seem to magically fall on all gardens visited by fairies.

A Midsummer
RECIPES
Night

Lemon-Blueberry Butterfly Bites

WHILE CHILDREN ENJOY THESE TINY WINGED CAKES, THE FAIRIES WILL MOST CERTAINLY NIBBLE ON WHAT'S LEFT ON YOUR SERVING PLATE!

MAKES 24 BUTTERFLY BITES

1⅓ cups sifted all-purpose flour
1 tsp. baking powder
½ tsp. baking soda
⅛ tsp. salt
½ tsp. cinnamon
⅛ tsp. nutmeg
4 Tbsp. (½ stick) unsalted butter
⅔ cup granulated sugar
2 large eggs
¾ cup sour cream
¾ cup frozen blueberries tossed with ¼ cup sugar (do not thaw)

Filling/Frosting

½ cup Lemon Curd (see page 62)
1 can whipped cream

Preheat oven to 350°F. Butter 2 dozen miniature muffin tins, or line with paper liners; set aside. Sift together flour, baking powder, baking soda, salt, cinnamon, and nutmeg. In a separate mixing bowl, cream butter until fluffy; beat in sugar. Add eggs 1 at a time, mixing well after each addition. Gradually beat in flour mixture until blended. Add sour cream and beat until incorporated. Fold in sugar-coated frozen berries and bake approximately 12–18 minutes. Remove from oven and turn out on racks immediately. Once completely cool, slice off rounded top of each mini muffin and reserve. Carefully scoop out a tiny bit of cake from muffin bottom and fill with 1–2 teaspoons of Lemon Curd. Pipe a swirl of whipped cream on top of filled cupcake. To form wings, slice each top in half, then push them at an angle into the whipped cream.

Fairies' Favorite Finger Sandwiches

....

BECAUSE FAIRIES LOVE FLOWERS, IT'S NO WONDER THEY'RE DRAWN TO THESE BEAUTIFUL LITTLE SANDWICHES. WATCH THEM DISAPPEAR...

MAKES 12 SANDWICHES

1 3-oz. package cream cheese, softened
1 Tbsp. lemon juice
2 Tbsp. orange juice
Grated zest of ½ lemon
Grated zest of ½ orange
24 slices thinly sliced white bread
1–2 packages (approximately 24) nasturtium flowers, pesticide free, petals chopped

In a small mixing bowl, combine cream cheese and juices. Beat with electric mixer at medium speed until smooth and fluffy. Stir in zests. Cut bread in rounds, and spread bread rounds with some of the cheese mixture. Top with additional slice of bread. Spread a thin layer of filling on edges. Roll round edge of sandwich in chopped nasturtium petals.

Enchanted Violet Jelly

....

OUR FRIEND MARGARET KLINGLER MAKES THIS JELLY FROM THE MAGNIFICENT VIOLETS SHE RAISES IN HER GARDEN. HER DELICIOUS RECIPE FOR THIS ROYAL-COLORED CONSERVE IS AN INSPIRATION TO THE GARDENER IN ALL OF US.

MAKES 8 SMALL JARS

1 quart purple violet flowers, firmly packed and pesticide free
Juice of 1 lemon
1 box fruit pectin
4 cups granulated sugar
Paraffin

Wash and pack violet flowers in a quart jar. Pour in enough boiling water to fill the jar and cover the violets. Place in the refrigerator overnight. Drain off 2 cups of liquid. Discard the violets. In medium saucepan combine violet liquid, lemon juice, and pectin. Bring to a boil, then add the sugar. Stir and bring to the boiling point. Boil 1 minute only. Skim if necessary and pour into 8 small sterilized baby food jars. Seal with melted paraffin.

Petal Scones

....

THESE DELICATE SCONES ARE PETAL-SHAPED. IDEALLY
SERVED WITH "DEVONSHIRE" CREAM (PAGE 62) AND
ENCHANTED VIOLET JELLY.
See The Queen's Cream Scones on page 16 for
recipe.

Flight-of-Fancy Fairy Cakes

....

ENGLISH LEGEND CONFIRMS THAT IF YOU LEAVE THESE
TINY UNGARNISHED CAKES OVERNIGHT IN THE GARDEN,
THEY WILL MAGICALLY APPEAR COVERED WITH TINY
FLOWERS IN THE MORNING. THIS RECIPE BY VICTORIA
ANDERSON IS A WELL-KNOWN FAVORITE AMONG THE FAIRY
COMMUNITY.

MAKES 20-30 FAIRY CAKES
Cake

> 3 large eggs, at room temperature
> 1 cup granulated sugar
> 5 Tbsp. milk
> 1 tsp. vanilla
> 1 cup all-purpose flour
> 1 tsp. baking powder
> ¼ tsp. salt

Frosting

> 8 Tbsp. (1 stick) butter, softened
> ½ – ¾ cup confectioners' sugar
> ¾ tsp. vanilla or strawberry extract

1–2 tsp. heavy cream or milk
Food coloring
Tiny leaves and flowers for decorating

For Cake
Preheat oven to 375° F. Grease and flour a jelly
roll pan. Beat eggs until thick and fluffy; gradually add sugar, beating well after each addition.
Beat in milk and vanilla. Mix together flour, baking powder, and salt; add to egg mixture and
beat until smooth. Spread batter into jelly roll
pan and bake 12–15 minutes. When cool, cut
into tiny shapes with miniature cookie cutters.

For Frosting
Mix butter and sugar together; add extract and
cream to give frosting good texture. Separate
into 4 bowls. Add 1 drop blue food coloring to
first bowl, 1 drop red to second, 1 drop green
to third, and 1 drop yellow to fourth. Fill 4

pastry bags (with different leaf and flower tips) with 1 color in each bag. Decorate each little cake with leaves and flowers.

Fairy Ring

Mushroom Meringues (see page 7) can also be used as a Fairy Ring for your table setting. To make a Fairy Ring, place meringues in a circle on your table, inserting a small Fairy Garden (page 53) or fairy-friendly flowers and plants, such as Johnny-jump-ups, pansies, or maidenhair fern inside the ring, along with small pebbles, moss, and acorn caps. When Fairy Beds (page 52) have been made, tuck each one under a mushroom cap so fairies can safely slumber.

Midsummer Fairy Punch with Frozen Flower Wreath

ALL OF YOUR ATTENDING GUESTS WILL LOVE THIS SPARKLING PUNCH TOPPED WITH A LOVELY FROZEN FLOWER WREATH. USE PESTICIDE-FREE, EDIBLE FLOWERS FROM YOUR GARDEN IN THE VIBRANT COLORS OF MIDSUMMER.

SERVES 12
Punch
  2–3 1.5-liter bottles raspberry ginger ale
  ½ pint fresh strawberries

Frozen Flower Wreath
  Select a combination of your favorites from the following, enough to fill a ring mold:
  Fresh woodruff leaves and flowers
  Fresh thyme
  Heartsease flowers
  Mint sprigs or lemon leaves
  Violets and violet leaves
  Strawberry flowers and small strawberry leaves

For Frozen Flower Wreath
Wash all flowers and fruit well. Fill a ring mold ¼ full with water and freeze. Lightly sprinkle with alternating flowers and greens on top of frozen ring; add enough water to just barely cover flowers. Rearrange if necessary. Freeze 1 hour. Repeat, adding another layer of flowers and water. Freeze 1 hour. When frozen, add water almost to the top and freeze 8 hours or overnight.

To unmold: Fill sink with hot water and dip ring mold halfway up to loosen. Lightly tap ring mold face-up on counter, then turn upside down and unmold onto a plate.

To serve: Place a glass punch bowl on the serving table. Chill the ginger ale and pour into the punch bowl. Hull strawberries and slice into the ginger ale. Set afloat the frozen flower wreath. Sprinkle surface of punch with additional heartsease, violets, and woodruff leaves. Sip and dream!

Victorian Party Activities

MAKING A DAISY CHAIN

Daisy chains were popular with Victorian girls, as fields of daisies were easy to find and the chains were easy to make. To fashion a daisy chain, cut daisies off at the stem in 3"–4" lengths. At 1" up from the bottom of the stem, with a small knife (or strong fingernail), make a small vertical ½"–¾" slice along the middle of the stem. Widen slice to easily slip the cut end of next daisy stem through the first sliced stem. Repeat until you have a chain of daisies long enough for a daisy crown or necklace. To finish off the chain, loop the final stem back through first stem slice.

MAKING A FAIRY BED

Fairies require special accommodations for their tiny sleeping quarters, as only natural materials and a certain blend of the elements make them drowsy enough to slumber in a place other than their very own fairy bed-room. To make a proper fairy bed, take half a walnut shell for the bed, a fuzzy green leaf for a blanket, and a pussy willow for a small fairy pillow. Line up the fairy beds at twilight in the garden, at the foot of your most fragrant flowers. In the morning, leaf blankets might be ruffled, indicating the fairies might have tossed and turned a little, but got a good night's sleep!

Tussie-Mussies and the Language of Flowers

The Victorians had a strong belief in *The Language of Flowers*, a philosophy that certain flowers represented different sentiments. Each flower was carefully selected by the romantic suitor and presented to his sweetheart, who then had a choice of how to accept the gift. If she chose not to wear the symbolic bloom, her message was clear; but if she pinned the flower close to her heart, the admirer was confident of her love. It became all the rage to fashion little ribbon-tied floral bouquets called "Tussie-Mussies," which were held in the hand by a small, horn-shaped vessel made of ivory, silver, or other metal.

PLANTING A FAIRY GARDEN

ine a basket (strawberry containers work well) with moss and fill with rich potting soil. Fairies love certain types of plants and flowers, including Johnny-jump-ups, pansies, and primroses. Add thyme, maidenhair fern, and alyssum, or any plants your fairies take a fancy to. Moss, lichens, small shells, and pebbles can be added to look like a carpet and fairy pathway. Keep in an area that gets bright morning sun, and water when the soil gets dry. Mist moss, lichens, and fern to keep them flourishing. Your fairies will love their own little garden, and will continue to bless *your* garden with an array of big, beautiful flowers!

Blessed with a Fairy Reward

t is a tradition that fairies leave a gold coin every night as a reward for special friends who keep their secrets. After your fairy tea, different types of fairy rewards can be left,

such as a miniature book, a package of fairy-friendly flower seeds, and a thimble or acorn cap, ideal receptacles from which thirsty fairies can drink their morning dew!

The Legend of the Witches' Ball

superstitious lot, the Victorians believed that the mirrorlike reflections found in a "witches' ball" encouraged good luck by confusing evil spirits and sending them speeding into the night. If you ever receive a witches' ball as a gift, you're in receipt of a legendary good luck charm. But beware! Never, ever, *sell* a witches' ball, as you will have just sold off your good luck.

THE HOLIDAY *Yuletide*

A FAMILY TEA

Lady dear, if Fairies may
For a moment lay aside
Cunning tricks and elfish play,
'Tis at happy Christmas-tide.

We have heard the children say—
Gentle children, whom we love—
Long ago, on Christmas Day,
Came a message from above.

Still, as Christmas-tide comes round,
They remember it again—
Echo still the joyful sound,
"Peace on earth, good-will to men!"

Yet the hearts must childlike be
Where such heavenly guests abide;
Unto children, in their glee,
All the year is Christmas-tide!

Thus, forgetting tricks and play
For a moment, Lady dear,
We would wish you, if we may,
Merry Christmas, glad New Year!

—*"FROM A FAIRY TO A CHILD"*
LEWIS CARROLL,
CHRISTMAS, 1867

a Family Tea at holiday time is a wonderful practice to embrace, and can be enjoyed when the hectic days of shopping are over and your family and friends have finally arrived.

Beginning this new holiday tradition can be fun for the family, yet few know that the Victorians were responsible for many of the customs we practice today.

In Victorian households, Christmas

wise for good luck. After each took their turn, a ring, a coin, and a silver thimble were tossed into the batter, which would then hang in a sack to mellow before being boiled in beef broth on Christmas Day. The person that bites into the ring will marry within the year; the coin brings wealth; and the thimble brings a happy, but single, life.

Traditions like this began in Victorian households, but probably the most signifi-

was more than just a holiday, it was a season of celebratory events. It began in late November on the first Sunday of Advent, when the Christmas pudding was mixed. Each family member would take a turn at beating the mixture, always stirring clock-

cant contribution was to make Christmas a family affair. An entire month was spent preparing foods and decorations. Advent calendars were painstakingly made and began on the 1st of December, counting down the days through December 24th. Bible verses and Christmas carols such as "Silent Night" and "O Christmas Tree" were sung by Victorian families every Advent Sunday, when a red candle would be lit for each in the Advent wreath, suspended above them as they sang.

Queen Victoria herself single-handedly brought the full-size Christmas tree into vogue. Before her reign, Christmas trees were strictly a tabletop item, modestly decorated with handmade ornaments. This tradition abruptly changed as her consort Prince Albert's German influence over Victoria began to flourish, and she adopted the custom of exhibiting a Christmas tree in the royal court. Once British loyal subjects saw the etching of their queen and

her royal family gathered around a large, ornate Christmas tree, well-to-do families had trees standing ten feet or more. Decorated on Christmas Eve, the Victorian tree supported heavy blown-glass globes, fragile shapes adorned with metallic wire, and three-dimensional cone-shaped paper ornaments filled with sweets. Thirty can-

Menu

SMOKED TURKEY WITH APPLE-
CRANBERRY MUFFINS
HERB MAYONNAISE
ORANGE-CURRANT SCONES
"CLOTTED" CREAM
LEMON CURD
ALICE'S FAVORITE
ORANGE MARMALADE
CHOCOLATEY COCONUT
MACAROONS
TRIFLE
FLAMING CHRISTMAS PUDDING
ENGLISH CREAM
MIMOSA PUNCH
SAINT NICHOLAS TEA

dles for each foot of tree were lit only twice during the holidays, on Christmas morning and New Year's Eve, for just twenty minutes at a time. Needless to say, a bucket filled with water with a long stick wrapped with a rag was never far from reach.

All things related to Christmas were popular with the Victorians. "The Night Before Christmas" was published in 1823, and is still read today as a Christmas Eve tradition. In the 1840s, in just six weeks, Charles Dickens wrote *A Christmas Carol*, his tale of Scrooge and how his lessons of Christmas Past, Present, and Future taught him the compassion that changed his life. In the 1880s, Christmas cards became fashionable, the more ornate the better. Elaborate cards decorated with lace, tinsel, puffy satin centers, feathers, glitter, fold-outs, and pop-ups were sent out by the dozens. Mistletoe was hung in every doorway, under which an unwary visitor was greeted with hugs and kisses. Parlor games provided an opportunity for Victorian children to have fun indoors, as this was the one time of the year that they could frolic in the parlor. They played Charades, enacting historical events that would amuse and entertain the family, sang Christmas carols, and enjoyed the sweets of the season.

The holidays were far from over once December 25th had passed. The ritual of

VICTORIAN CHRISTMAS Traditions

SINGING CHRISTMAS CAROLS

CHRISTMAS CRACKERS

"SAVING FOUR"

CHRISTMAS PARLOR GAMES

the Yule log was a tradition everyone treasured: the largest log of wood a family member could find was decorated with sprigs of holly and then lit in the fireplace, in hopes that it would continue to burn throughout the twelve days of Christmas. Boxing Day, which falls on December 26th, commemorates the Feast of Saint Stephen, the first Christian martyr. To honor this day, employers gave their servants boxes of food and gifts to bring home to their families, and on this day, alms boxes are sent to the poor. Twelfth Night, January 6th, is the Feast of Epiphany, and symbolizes the day when the Three Kings arrived in Bethlehem with their gifts of gold, frankincense, and myrrh for the Christ Child.

We owe many of our holiday traditions to the Victorians. The most important is the value of family participation in all we prepare for, in all we celebrate. At this special time of year, create memories for your children that they can someday pass down to their own. It is remarkable that so many of the Christmas customs we enjoy today began more than one hundred years ago. It is up to all of us to carry on these rituals of our most important season. In remembering the old, we create the new.

The Holiday Yuletide

RECIPES

Apple-Cranberry Muffins

AT TEATIME DURING THE HOLIDAYS, SPREAD THESE DELICIOUS
FRUIT-FILLED MUFFINS WITH FRAGRANT HERB MAYONNAISE
(PAGE 61) AND STUFF WITH SMOKED TURKEY.

MAKES 12 MUFFINS

1¾ cups all-purpose flour
½ cup granulated sugar
1½ tsp. baking powder
½ tsp. baking soda
½ tsp. salt
1 large egg
¾ cup milk
¾ cup sweetened applesauce
4 Tbsp. (½ stick) butter, melted
1 cup fresh cranberries, coarsely
  chopped
2 Tbsp. all-purpose flour

Preheat oven to 400°F. Grease 12 muffin cups; set aside. In a medium bowl, combine flour, sugar, baking powder, baking soda, and salt. In a small bowl, combine egg, milk, applesauce, and butter; mix well. Add egg mixture to flour mixture, stirring just until moistened—batter will be lumpy. In another small bowl, toss chopped cranberries with remaining 2 Tbsp. flour; fold into batter. Spoon batter into muffin cups. Bake 20–25 minutes. Remove from oven and cool on wire racks.

For Muffins Stuffed with Smoked Turkey: Slice all 12 muffins in half and spread with Herb Mayonnaise. Stuff with thinly sliced smoked turkey. (½ lb. smoked turkey will fill 12 muffins.)

Herb Mayonnaise

IN A DIVINE SHADE OF GREEN, THIS IS A FLAVORFUL ACCOMPANIMENT TO MANY SAVORY SANDWICHES, ESPECIALLY APPLE-CRANBERRY MUFFINS (PAGE 60) STUFFED WITH SMOKED TURKEY.

MAKES 3 CUPS
> ½ lb. fresh spinach, stems removed
> 2 Tbsp. coarsely chopped shallots
> ¼ cup watercress leaves
> ¼ cup chopped fresh parsley
> 2 Tbsp. fresh tarragon leaves
> 2½ cups mayonnaise (Best Foods, Hellmann's, or homemade)

Bring 3 cups water to a boil as you prepare greens. Place spinach, shallots, watercress, parsley, and tarragon in a pot. Cover with the boiling water; steep 1 minute. Drain, then place greens in several layers of paper toweling and wring out until dry. Add drained greens to a food processor and chop until fine. Quickly stir in mayonnaise. Chill in refrigerator until ready to serve. Can also be used as a dip for vegetables. Keeps in the refrigerator up to 3 days.

Orange-Currant Scones

THESE OH-SO-RICH, ORANGE-SCENTED SCONES ARE EVERYONE'S FAVORITE AT HOLIDAY TIME. THEY ARE POSITIVELY LUSCIOUS SLATHERED WITH BUTTER, THICK "CLOTTED" CREAM (PAGE 62) AND PRESERVES, OR A SPOONFUL OF LEMON CURD (PAGE 62).

MAKES 3½ DOZEN 2" SCONES
> 6 cups self-rising flour
> ½ cup sugar
> ¾ lb. (3 sticks) unsalted butter, softened
> 5 oz. (½ cup [heaping]) currants
> 3 Tbsp. grated orange peel
> 1½ cups milk
> Additional milk for brushing

Preheat oven to 450°F. Grease a baking sheet; set aside. In a *very* large bowl, mix together the flour, sugar, and butter and work into a mixture that resembles coarse cornmeal. Add currants and orange peel. (If you wish to make ahead, the dough can be refrigerated at this point.) Then add milk and mix well. Turn out onto a floured board and pat the dough until it holds together, handling as little as possible. Roll out to ¾" thickness and cut with 2" round cutter. Place on greased baking sheet and brush tops with milk. Bake 7–10 minutes, until tops are browned.

"Clotted" Cream

MAKE THIS SUMPTUOUS "CLOTTED" CREAM WHENEVER YOU BAKE SCONES. IT MAKES ALL THE DIFFERENCE.

MAKES 1½ CUPS—SERVES 4–6
1 cup heavy cream
2 Tbsp. confectioners' sugar
½ cup sour cream, at room temperature

In a small bowl, using an electric mixer, combine heavy cream and sugar. Whip until stiff peaks form. Gently fold in sour cream and mix until very thick. Place in refrigerator and chill until time to serve. If made ahead of time, it will keep in the refrigerator up to 4 hours.

"Devonshire" Cream

JUST SLIGHTLY DIFFERENT FROM BUT JUST AS DELECTABLE AS "CLOTTED" CREAM ABOVE. SERVE COLD WITH WARM, HEART-SHAPED SCONES.

MAKES 2¼ CUPS
1 8-oz. package cream cheese
1 tsp. vanilla
3 Tbsp. granulated sugar
¼ cup sour cream
¼ cup whipping cream

(All ingredients should be at room temperature)

Beat cream cheese with an electric mixer until fluffy, then beat in remaining ingredients until well blended. Cover and refrigerate until serving time. Spoon into a pretty bowl and serve.

Lemon Curd

EASY TO MAKE AND DELIGHTFULLY FRESH-TASTING, OUR FAVORITE IS SLIGHTLY MORE SWEET THAN MANY TART LEMON CURDS FOUND IN A JAR.

MAKES 2 CUPS
Zest of 2 large lemons, finely grated
Juice from 2 large lemons, strained to remove pulp and seeds
1⅓ cups granulated sugar
3 large eggs, slightly beaten
5⅓ Tbsp. (⅓ cup) unsalted butter

In the top of a double boiler, combine lemon zest, strained juice, sugar, and eggs. Lightly whisk together until well blended, about 30 seconds. Place pan over simmering water and cook, stirring constantly, until thickened and smooth, about 5 minutes. Do not allow mixture to boil. Remove the top of the double boiler from the hot water and stir in the butter, a little at a time, until blended. Mixture will continue to thicken as it cools in the refrigerator. Store in a container covered with a lid or plastic wrap to keep a film from forming. Chill thoroughly (3 hours) until ready to serve. This will keep for up to 1 week in the refrigerator.

Alice's Favorite Orange Marmalade

··

THIS RECIPE IS ALICE LIDDELL'S OWN, WRITTEN IN THE LATE 1800S AND GIVEN TO US BY HER GRANDDAUGHTER, MARY JEAN ST. CLAIR.

Take 1 dozen Seville oranges, put them into a large pan of water, boil them gently 2 or 3 hours in two waters until quite tender. Drain them. Take out the pips only. Slice the fruit very fine, boil well for half an hour with 2 lbs. of loaf sugar and half a pint of fresh water to every lb. of fruit.

The first boiling may be done the day previously. If the marmalade is preferred bitter, the water that the oranges were first boiled in can be used instead of fresh water.* 1 dozen oranges will make 8 common 12 oz. jars of marmalade. *Note: *Fresh water* was always used for Grandmama's marmalade, which was what we liked.

—MARY JEAN ST. CLAIR,
ALICE'S GRANDDAUGHTER

Chocolatey Coconut Macaroons

··

THE PERFECT PAIRING OF COCONUT AND CHOCOLATE. BAKING THESE ON A LAYER OF PARCHMENT PAPER ASSURES THEY WON'T STICK, AND USING AN AIR-SANDWICHED COOKIE SHEET PREVENTS THE BOTTOMS FROM BURNING.

MAKES 3 DOZEN
⅔ cup all-purpose flour
5 cups shredded sweetened coconut
¼ tsp. salt
⅔ cup (14-oz. can) sweetened condensed milk
1 tsp. vanilla extract
For decoration: 3–4 oz. semisweet chocolate, melted

Preheat oven to 325°F. Line a cookie sheet with parchment paper, or grease pan well. Mix flour, coconut, and salt in a bowl. Add sweetened condensed milk and vanilla; stir well. Drop in large rounded spoonfuls onto cookie sheet, allowing enough room for cookies to spread. Bake 20–25 minutes, or until golden brown. Remove macaroons from pan at once; place cookies on racks, sliding used parchment paper under racks.

To decorate: Melt chocolate over double boiler. Drizzle chocolate back and forth over top of macaroons, or dip ½ macaroon in chocolate and return to racks.

Trifle

....

A SPECIAL "ADULT" DESSERT YOUR PARTY GUESTS WILL LOVE, THIS SUMPTUOUS TRIFLE INCORPORATES A BRANDY-FLAVORED VANILLA FILLING AMID LAYERS OF SOFT CAKE, CREAM, AND BERRIES. IF SERVING CHILDREN, SIMPLY ELIMINATE THE ALCOHOL.

SERVES 12

3.4-oz. package instant vanilla pudding
1½ cups half-and-half
¼ cup brandy or sherry
3¼ cups whipping cream
5 Tbsp. granulated sugar
2 Tbsp. red raspberry preserves
10" round sponge cake layer or 1 angel food cake
¼ cup brandy
¼ cup sherry
1 bag frozen mixed berries, thawed and drained, or 30 fresh strawberries

2–3 Tbsp. red raspberry preserves or tube of red decorating gel (for top)
Fresh raspberries or strawberries for garnish

To make filling: Lightly whisk together pudding mix and half-and-half. Mix in brandy or sherry. Chill filling thoroughly. Whip cream and sugar until stiff; measure 1¼ cups of whipped cream and fold into chilled filling mixture. Keep remaining whipped cream in refrigerator until ready to decorate top.

To assemble: Using a brush, coat bottom and sides of a deep, 10" diameter Trifle bowl with raspberry preserves to within 1" of top of bowl. Slice sponge cake horizontally into fourths. Place top slice, crust side up, in bottom of preserves-coated bowl, curving outer edge to layer upward. Combine brandy and sherry and sprinkle 2 Tbsp. over the cake layer. Next, spread ⅓ of the chilled filling mixture over the surface. Repeat procedure with 2 additional cake layers. Finish by pouring mixed berries on the top of third layer of filling and cover with a fourth cake layer, crust side down. Sprinkle with remaining brandy-sherry mixture.

To decorate: Thinly frost the top of the cake layer with a few large spoonfuls of the reserved whipped cream. Cut off tip of red decorating gel, or fill a small pastry bag fitted with a small writing tube (or make a paper cone with tip cut to make ⅛" diameter hole) and pipe raspberry preserves in parallel lines, ½" apart. Draw tip of knife across lines at ½" intervals, alternating first in one direction and then in the other. Place remaining whipped cream in pastry bag fitted with a fluted tip. Pipe swirls of whipped cream around edge of the bowl. Refrigerate at least 2 hours. When ready to serve, top each swirl with a fresh berry. Spoon onto chilled dessert plates.

Flaming Christmas Pudding

ANY PURCHASED PLUM PUDDING CAN BE FESTIVELY TRIMMED AND THEN SET ABLAZE TO TAKE CENTER STAGE. SERVE THE SLICED PUDDING NAPPED IN A POOL OF SMOOTH ENGLISH CREAM (SEE NEXT COLUMN).

SERVES 12
1 purchased large plum pudding
½ cup rum or whiskey, heated
Holly sprigs

To steam the pudding: Follow package instructions or follow these: At least 2 hours before you plan to serve, remove all cellophane wrapping from pudding, ensuring that the plastic lid is securely fastened to the mold. Place mold, *lid side up*, in a large soup kettle. Fill with water to half the depth of the pudding mold. Boil 2 hours (or according to package directions), checking so it will not boil dry. Remove pudding immediately from kettle, remove lid, and unmold onto a *hot* flameproof serving platter. Decorate with holly sprigs.

To ignite: Pour the heated rum or whiskey around the warm pudding and ignite. When the flame subsides, slice and serve with English Cream (below). Note: To assure successful flaming, the pudding must be very warm!

English Cream

THIS ENGLISH CREAM (COMMONLY KNOWN AS CRÈME ANGLAISE) IS FLAVORED WITH A HINT OF LEMON, A LAVISHLY DELICATE COMPLEMENT TO THE DENSE AND MELLOW CHRISTMAS PLUM PUDDING.

MAKES 2 CUPS
7 large egg yolks
⅔ cup granulated sugar
1½ cups hot milk
1 Tbsp. vanilla extract
3 Tbsp. unsalted butter
1 tsp. lemon zest, finely grated

Beat egg yolks in a saucepan, then add sugar by large spoonfuls until incorporated. Continue beating about 3 minutes, until mixture thickens and turns a pale yellow. Gradually pour in the milk a little at a time, and stir. Set saucepan over low heat, and stir slowly until it comes *near* a simmer. When it is almost ready, tiny bubbles will begin to disappear and steam will begin to rise. Sauce will be ready when a thick layer coats the back of a wooden spoon. Remove from heat and beat in vanilla, butter, and grated lemon zest. Serve warm with Christmas pudding.

Mimosa Punch

A BEAUTIFUL PUNCH FOR THE ADULTS, REMINISCENT OF THE VICTORIAN WASSAIL.

SERVES 12

Cinnamon-Sugar Syrup
⅓ cup granulated sugar
3 2½" cinnamon sticks
½ cup water

Punch
1 quart orange juice
¼ cup orange-flavored liqueur
¼ cup brandy
1 liter bottle sparkling water, chilled
1 750ml bottle champagne, chilled

Punch Bowl Garnish
Green, red, and purple grapes
3 large egg whites
Sugar for coating
Greens and ribbons

To make the syrup: In a 1-quart saucepan over high heat, heat sugar, cinnamon sticks, and ½ cup water to a boil. Reduce heat to low; cover and simmer 15 minutes. Refrigerate.

To make punch bowl garnish: Clip large grape clusters into small bunches; dip in egg white and then in sugar. Refrigerate.

To serve: Place 6-quart punch bowl on large, decorative tray. Add the orange juice, liqueur, brandy, and syrup and mix. Stir in sparkling water and champagne. Decorate around punch bowl base and tray with festive ribbon, greens, and frosted grapes.

Nonalcoholic substitute: Eliminate all alcoholic ingredients and add 2 cups pineapple juice and 1 2-liter bottle ginger ale, chilled.

Victorian Christmas Traditions

SINGING CHRISTMAS CAROLS

The Victorians were great music lovers, and sang at any and all social occasions. "Silent Night" and "O Christmas Tree" were made popular by the Victorians, who brought back the medieval custom of singing carols. Published in 1871, *Christmas Carols Old and New* featured "The First Noel" (at that time, 400 years old), "Hark, the Herald Angels Sing" (then nearly 150 years old), and "O Holy Night." When you sing these songs this holiday season, you'll be singing songs that were on the lips of your ancestors hundreds of years ago, an important tradition handed down from one generation to the next.

Christmas Crackers

The Victorians loved Christmas crackers, and today the brightly wrapped paper cylinders filled with a paper hat, balloon, fortune, and little toy are readily available at holiday time. According to custom, after the main course was finished at Queen Victoria's table and before the Christmas pudding arrived, a Christmas cracker, placed at each setting, was pulled apart at each end, which made a loud pop or cracking sound, and inside, gifts were found to amuse while awaiting the grand finale of the flaming Christmas pudding. To avoid the temptation of early "Christmas cracking," hand these out just after the dinner plates have been cleared.

"SAVING FOUR"

A Christmas Eve tradition in many Victorian households was that of removing four presents from their collection under the tree. One was to be opened the day after Christmas, for Boxing Day, in honor of the

Feast of Saint Stephen, the first Christian martyr. Boxing Day gets its name from the distribution of alms boxes for the poor, and the one day of the year when servants would take home to their families boxes of food and gifts from their employers. The other three presents were to be opened on Twelfth Night—January 6th, the Feast of Epiphany. These presents represent the three gifts of the Magi, the Three Kings who came from the East and arrived in Bethlehem with gold, frankincense, and myrrh for the Christ Child.

Christmas Parlor Games

CHARADES

This is the ideal game once the family has eaten and has retired from the dining room. Place folded pieces of paper in a hat, with a Christmas saying, name of a holiday song, Christmas carol, or (in the case of the Victorians) a historical event written on each one. Each player will have five minutes to enact their appointed task, with the player not allowed to speak any words, including yes or no! Each seated participant calls out what the player is enacting; the first one to guess the task wins, and takes his or her turn at Charades. As each person takes a turn, they choose another piece of paper out of the hat before returning to the "stage."

ANIMAL, VEGETABLE, OR MINERAL

It's surprising how many games stand the test of time, including the Victorian favorite, Animal, Vegetable, or Mineral. To play, each person selects a certain animal, vegetable, or mineral and commits it to memory. The other players have a total of 20 yes-or-no questions they can ask the player. One begins by asking, "Are you an animal?" If the answer is yes, they can ask another question. If the answer is no, the next player asks, "Are you a vegetable?" And so on, until all 20 questions are asked. If the mystery is never solved, the winning player chooses another animal, vegetable, or mineral, and the game begins again.

Acknowledgments

We would like to thank many people for helping us with this book. To Sunday Hendrickson, for her hard work, cheerful disposition, and ability to realize our vision; to Kathryn Russell, for her commitment to perfection; and to her assistants Kevin Naifeh and Joakim Blomdahl, who kept on smiling even though the light would inevitably change the moment we went to film; to Diane Elander for making our food look beautiful; to Melody Barnett for clothing our party guests in the best of vintage attire; and for the exquisite Yuletide clothing, thank you to Sandra Johnson. To Edward Wakeling and Anne Clark Amor for generously taking the time to write the Foreword; and to Darlene Jones for her lovely illustrations. To Lois and Gerry Ludwig (and Frank—thanks so much for all your help), Randy and Diana Ema, Jeri Cunningham, and Linda and Peter Gartner for providing our beautiful locations and allowing us into their lives during our photo shoots; to Mary Jean St. Clair for driving to Oxford to locate the recipe for Alice's marmalade; to David and Maxine Schaefer and David and Denise Carlson of the Lewis Carroll Society for helping to clarify information about Alice. A special thank-you to Julie Creasy for her wonderful handmade Cheshire Cat Grin; to Margaret Klingler for sending us her Violet Jelly; and to Barbara, Mary, and Betty Jean Dyvig for their creative ideas, their love for the charms of tea, and Betty's handcrafted ceramics that inspired the project.

To our friends at the Victorian Tea Society for monthly doses of inspiration; to Sarah Ban Breathnach for answering numerous questions about customs while trying to meet her own deadline for *Simple Abundance*; to longtime friends Julie Palmer, Cindy Bonner, and Nancy Reese for their support and belief in this project; to Devin and Colin Sedo for their loving patience; to Harold Mitchell for watching the boys during scouting missions and errands and, of course, for getting the trailer to our first outdoor photo shoot; and to Betty Mitchell, may this book be a loving remembrance. To all of our young party guests: Devin, Sierra, Devon, Manhattan, Cailin, Alexandra, Nathaniel, Paisley, Felicity, Charlotte, Hannah, Maya, Mary Claire, Czara, Christian, Zoe, and Brandon: you were terrific, and we hope you enjoyed the experience.

To Jennifer Currie for her inspiration and ideas, a dear friend who has been giving tea parties for years; to Weatherly Gottlieb, for her hours of input about how much fun a tea party should be; to Jerry Gold for his welcome legal advice; to Odessa Hylton for her family recipes and hours of encouragement to us both; and to Everett Hylton, for his advice and confidence. We would also like to send a special thank-you to our editor, Amye Dyer of Warner Treasures, for her level head and words of assurance; and to Madelaine M. Netter, without whose steadfast support and firm belief in the project this book might have never been published. Last but not least, a special thank-you to our families and a big debt of gratitude to our husbands, Barry Gottlieb and Bob Sedo: they endured a continuous torrent of recipe testing, tearoom outings, and quests for the perfect addition to the table setting. To all of you, thank you from the bottom of our hearts.

Source Guide

Dedication: Teacups by Betty Jean Dyvig exclusively for Angels Garden Designs, 486 El Camino Real, Tustin, CA 92780, (714) 669-1337.

Alice's Adventures in Wonderland by Lewis Carroll: Alice Hargreaves copy, from the Harnsworth collection, illustrated in color by Margaret Tarrant (1918) and signed: "Alice Pleasance Hargreaves," author owned. Books like these available through: D & D Galleries, Box 8413, Somerville, NJ 08876, (908) 874-3162, fax (908) 874-5195. *A wonderful source for one-of-a-kind and limited-edition books.*

Drink Me: Tea with the Mad Hatter: garden site courtesy of Diana & Randy Ema, Santa Ana, CA.

Selected MacKenzie-Childs serveware: courtesy of The Cubby Hole, Dolores St. between Ocean & 7th, Carmel, CA 93921, (408) 624-9595. *A warm welcome to the wonderland world of MacKenzie-Childs.*

Selected antiques: courtesy of Santa Monica Antique Market, 1607 Lincoln Blvd., Santa Monica, CA 90404, (310) 314-4899. *An excellent source of antiques from every era.*

Reaching-Through-the-House Dollhouse: courtesy of Petite Designs, 10523 Santa Monica Blvd., Los Angeles, CA 90025, (310) 477-9388. *For the most beautiful hand-painted dollhouses ever made.*

All vintage clothing courtesy of Melody Barnett of Palace Costume Company, 835 N. Fairfax, Los Angeles, CA, (213) 651-5458. *An excellent source for Victorian and vintage clothing from every era. Open to the trade only.*

Edible flowers: courtesy of Malibu Farms, 5743 Smithway, Commerce, CA 90040, (213) 278-9750. *For a wide variety of fresh herbs and edible flowers.*

Painting the Roses Red: Tea in the Garden: garden site courtesy of Linda & Peter Gartner, Orange, CA.

Victoriana of the Romantic Kind: Tea Leaf Cottage, 60 Plaza Square, Orange, CA 92666, (714) 771-7752. *Antiques, gifts, and collectibles.*

The Coronation of Queen Alice: A Nursery Tea: garden site courtesy of Jeri Cunningham, Orange, CA.

The Coronation of Queen Alice: A Nursery Tea: all tea sets, napkin rings, and Talking Flower by Betty Jean Dyvig exclusively for Angels Garden Designs, 486 El Camino Real, Tustin, CA 92780, (714) 669-1337. *This specialty shop is an ideal source for antique and vintage linens, lace, tea accoutrements, and unique one-of-a-kind gifts.*

Selected vintage tablecloths, pillows, and furniture: courtesy of Vintage & Cottage Interiors, 139 N. Harwood Street, Orange, CA 92666, (714) 563-6013.

Selected china, serveware, and Victorian accoutrements at Cupid's Tea and Holiday Yuletide Tea: courtesy of Pocketful of Roses Antiques, 10864 Kling Street, Toluca Lake, CA 91602, (818) 755-0900. *A wonderful little shop that specializes in antique china and silver.*

Victorian silver basket: courtesy of Robin Leffler, Antique Annex, 109 S. Glassell, Orange, CA 92666, (714) 997-4320. *A variety of antiques from every era.*

Frozen Charlotte: available at Martha's China Cupboard, Treasure Mart, 293 E. Redlands Blvd., San Bernardino, CA 92408, (909) 825-7264. *An incredible selection of Victorian dolls, collectibles, pickle castors, and silverware.*

Victorian stickers and gift wrap: The Gifted Line, 999 Canal Blvd., Point Richmond, CA 94804, 1-800-5-GIFTED. *For a beautiful selection of Victorian stationery items, gift wrapping, and stickers.*

A Midsummer Night: Tea with the Fairies: garden site courtesy of Linda & Peter Gartner, Orange, CA.

Tussie-Mussies: handmade by Leslie Munro Grenier, courtesy of Heard's Country Garden, 14391 Edwards Street, Westminster, CA 92683, (714) 894-2444. *Garden-fresh herbs, plants, and flowers of all varieties.*

Witches' Ball: courtesy of Alan Townsend, Tustin Consignments, 474 El Camino Real, Tustin, CA 92780, (714) 730-5037. *Furniture and fine accessories.*

Fairy-friendly: Heart's Ease Herb Shop & Gardens, 4101 Burton Dr., Cambria, CA 93428, (805) 927-5224 or (800) 266-HERB (4372). *For all things fairy-related, this is the place. Host of the annual Faerie Festival, last Sunday in April.*

Fairy-friendly: The Proper Season, 155 Chestnut Ave., Andover, MA 01801, (508) 470-0911. *An excellent source for the fairy gardener in all of us.*

Handmade fairy wreath (not pictured): available from Barbara Malmin of Garden Memories, 28 S. California St., Ventura, CA 93001, (805) 641-1070. *For the most beautiful one-of-a-kind handmade wreaths.*

Yuletide holiday clothing: designed and handmade by Sandra Johnson, 138 S. Robertson Blvd., Los Angeles, CA 90048, (310) 247-8206. *Very special clothing for very special occasions.*

Victorian celebrations: Mrs. Sharp's Traditions® by Sarah Ban Breathnach (see Bibliography). "A month-by-month guide to creating seasonal feasts, traditional crafts, and the little daily rituals that make a house a home." *The single most comprehensive book on Victorian celebrations available.*

Lewis Carroll Society of North America: To become a member, contact LCSNA Secretary Ellie Luchinsky, 18 Fitzharding Pl., Owings Mills, MD 21117.

The Lewis Carroll Society: To join the Society, contact Sarah Stanfield, Acorns, Dargate, Near Faversham, Kent, ME13 9HG, England. Members receive a quarterly journal, *Jabberwocky*; a regular newsletter, *Bandersnatch*; and other occasional publications.

Recipe Credits

Lemon-Raspberry Looking-Glass Cake: from the original recipe entitled "Lemon-Raspberry Cake," courtesy of Sweet Lady Jane Tearoom, 8360 Melrose Ave., Los Angeles, CA, (213) 653-7145.

Midsummer Fairy Punch with Frozen Flower Wreath & Flight-of-Fancy Fairy Cakes: from the original recipes entitled "Faerie Punch, Floral Ice Ring & Fairy Cakes," in *Are There Faeries at the Bottom of Your Garden?* by Betsy Williams (see Bibliography).

Shortbread Crowns: from the original "Scotch Shortbread" Liddell family recipe, courtesy of Sandra Liddell Pasqua.

The Queen's Cream Scones, "Clotted" Cream & Saint Valentine's Pound Cake: recipes courtesy of Odessa Hylton.

Enchanted Violet Jelly: recipe courtesy of Margaret Klingler.

Apple-Cranberry Muffins & Herb Mayonnaise: recipes courtesy of Sue Lortie.

Orange-Currant Scones: recipe courtesy of Trisha Tallman.

Alice's Favorite Orange Marmalade: from the original Liddell family recipe, courtesy of Mary Jean St. Clair, Alice's only grandchild.

Bibliography

Beeton, Isabella. *Mrs. Beeton's Victorian Cookbook*. Topsfield, Mass.: Salem House Publishers, 1988. (Originally titled *Beeton's Book of Household Management*, London, 1836–1865.)

Bjork, Christina. *The Other Alice: The Story of Alice Liddell and Alice in Wonderland*. Illustrated by Inga-Karin Eriksson. Stockholm: R & S Books, 1993.

Breathnach, Sarah Ban. *Mrs. Sharp's Traditions*. New York: Simon & Schuster, 1990. (Also titled *Victorian Family Celebrations*.)

Carroll, Lewis. *The Best of Lewis Carroll*. Secaucus, NJ: Book Sales, Inc., 1992.

———. *Through the Looking Glass and What Alice Found There*. New York: William Morrow & Co., 1993. (Originally published by Macmillan & Co., London, 1872.)

Clark, Anne. *Lewis Carroll: A Biography*. New York: Schocken Books, 1979.

———. *The Real Alice*. New York: Stein & Day, 1981.

Gardner, Martin, ed. *More Annotated Alice*. New York: Random House, 1990.

Hart, Cynthia, John Grossman, and Priscilla Dunhill. *Joy to the World: A Victorian Christmas*. New York: Workman Publishing, 1990.

Laufer, Geraldine Adamich. *Tussie-Mussies: The Victorian Art of Expressing Yourself in the Language of Flowers*. New York: Workman Publishing, 1993.

Leopold, Alison Kyle. *Victorian Sweets*. New York: Clarkson N. Potter, 1992.

Lovejoy, Sharon. *Faeries in My Garden*. N.p., 1994.

Wakeling, Edward, ed. *Lewis Carroll's Diaries*. Lewis Carroll Society. Oxford: The Lewis Carroll Birthplace Trust, 1993–96.

———. *Lewis Carroll's Games & Puzzles*. New York: Dover, 1992.

———. *Rediscovered Lewis Carroll Puzzles*. New York: Dover, 1993.

Williams, Betsy. *Are There Faeries at the Bottom of Your Garden?* N.p., 1994.